P. 28 - natural [...]

P. 38 - in containers [...]

P. 53 - Chinese Pickled Beets

P. 96 - Green Goddess dressing

THE BEGINNER'S KITCHEN GARDEN

THE
BEGINNER'S
KITCHEN
GARDEN

by jan riemer

Drawings by Lauren Jarrett

WILLIAM MORROW AND COMPANY, INC.
NEW YORK 1975

My appreciation to those who generously shared their
pet recipes:
My mother, Mildred Perkins Ludwig
Kay Barndt
Lucille Hall
Olena Ludwig
Carol Mason
Fay Scherr
Jean Smith

Printed in the United States of America.

Library of Congress Cataloging in Publication Data

Riemer, Jan.
  The beginner's kitchen garden.

  1. Vegetable gardening.   2. Organic gardening.
I. Title.
SB321.R54   635   75-752
ISBN 0-688-02921-3
ISBN 0-688-07921-0 pbk.

Book design: Helen Roberts

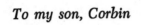

To my son, Corbin

CONTENTS

Introduction   9

part i: sowing

GARDEN PREPARATION   15
COMPANION PLANTING   27
STARTING SEEDS INDOORS   31
CONTAINER GARDENING   37

part ii: reaping

BEANS   43
BEETS   51
CABBAGE   55
CARROTS   61
CUCUMBERS   65
HERBS   69
LETTUCE   87
ONIONS   91
PEAS   99
PEPPERS   105
RADISHES   109
SPINACH   113
SQUASH   117
TOMATOES   125
Index   131

INTRODUCTION

Not since World War II has there been such a pro-
liferation of home gardens as today—and no wonder!
Soaring produce prices and tasteless supermarket vegetables make the idea of raising one's own more and more
attractive. Our heightened awareness of the world's
energy, ecological, and food problems demands that we
look for ways to conserve natural resources and make our-
selves, individually and nationally, more self-sufficient.

Everyone can grow a vegetable garden. Size is in-
cidental. Even a small patch can be made amazingly
productive. Apartment dwellers with a sunny balcony,
windowsill, or porch can raise miniature gardens supplying many types of vegetables, salad ingredients, and
herbs. Front lawns can be converted into well-designed
food gardens. Vegetable plantings imaginatively inter-
spersed with flowers such as marigolds, nasturtiums, geraniums, and painted daisies *(Pyrethrum roseum)* create
pleasing and practical effects. Just visualize a neat row of
tomato plants, and instead of going out to dig crabgrass
and dandelions, going out to pick part of your dinner!

This book is for the beginning gardener and hopefully will eliminate the frustrations and disappointments of incomplete or misguided information which often besiege the novice. The step-by-step minicourse in organic vegetable gardening is supplemented by tips and shortcuts not included in the usual garden book. These should eliminate hours of research and confusion and put you on the road to becoming an expert in the art of gardening. Once you taste a snow pea fresh from your very own vine, you'll be hooked forever. And you'll be embarked on a hobby that will bring years of enjoyment into your life as well as the dividends of unsurpassed vegetables on your table.

The virtues of organic gardening are many. You won't have to resort to the use of poisonous pesticides, which are hazardous and destructive to our atmosphere, population, birds, insects, and animals, and you will also be rewarded by tastier, healthier vegetables. Organic materials increase the nutrient values of the soil and encourage the invasion of worms, bees, toads, ladybugs, praying mantises, and birds—all important to a healthy garden.

Our first years of gardening were not organic. The contrast between the results we obtained then and what we achieve now is almost unbelievable. We discovered, for example, that the best way of controlling pests and diseases is to prevent their attack, and that's just what organic methods do.

The Beginner's Kitchen Garden is divided into two parts. The first deals with how to select a site, prepare the soil, choose companion plants, start seeds indoors, and grow vegetables in containers. Two sample plans of crops for a 13- by 13-foot garden and two for a 10- by 16-foot garden are included. The second section describes the care and culture of common, easy-to-grow vegetables and herbs in alphabetical order. And because we Americans have such a reputation for waste, the chapters on each vegetable suggest appropriate storage procedures for garden surplus along with recipes using stored vegetables.

Many vegetables can be stored in a slatted basket with dry sand between the layers. Those that cannot be preserved this way can be frozen or canned (freezing generally is faster and results in better flavor). But if you don't have much freezer space, a basic hot-pack method of canning is described on page 48, and this method can be used with other vegetables. Food that is not preserved properly can be poisonous, so be extremely careful to follow the manufacturer's directions that come with jars purchased for preserving, or consult a good cookbook. Herbs are easily dried for storage, and this is discussed on page 70.

Many vegetables are not included in this beginning guide because they demand too much space and/or technical know-how. But once you have learned from your first garden, you can add corn, asparagus, and celery; experiment with eggplant, potatoes, and broccoli. You can become a crafty gardener—planting what you and your family like best, and what is most expensive to buy.

The joys of gardening cannot be exaggerated. If you have been in the rut of salads made only of lettuce and tomato, you'll discover a whole new world of succulent salad greens that can serve as a main dish with the addition of proteins such as cheese, meat, shellfish, or beans. Spinach used instead of lettuce changes the whole quality of a salad.

Vegetables picked just before cooking offer flavors you have never savored before. Quick blanching (i.e., scalding) of freshly picked produce locks in valuable vitamins and minerals. Salad dressings pepped up with the addition of home-grown herbs give salads a unique and special flavor. And sunlight filtering through bottles of vinegar steeping with branches of tarragon can turn a kitchen windowsill into a Norman Rockwell painting.

Physically and mentally the benefits of gardening cannot be matched. Muscles that have been dormant are put to use. The vitamin and mineral content of freshly picked vegetables is much higher than that in the stale supermarket varieties that are days—even weeks—from their sources. Many dollars can be saved, and a peaceful tranquillity will permeate your spirit as you watch the little seeds sprout and mature because *you* planted and *you* nurtured them.

Even considering the initial investment in tools, soil additives, and seeds, the potential savings the first year can be worthwhile. Seeds for sample garden plans cost about five dollars at this writing, and would yield over one hundred dollars' worth of fresh vegetables.

It is a joy for me to share my knowledge with you. But I must assure you (out of years of experience) that no garden is ever as perfect as you could wish. Hail, heavy rains, unusually hot or cold weather, the absence of sun—any of these conditions can deliver crushing blows to the most conscientious gardener. So don't despair!

While tending or admiring my garden, I'm often reminded of Thoreau's deep sensitivity to nature, and how few of us twentieth-century mortals have the opportunity to share his feelings. Industrial progress has brought undeniable benefits, but has also caused serious human and environmental imbalances. These can be partially corrected through our individual gardening adventures that stimulate each of our senses with an awareness we might not otherwise have known—and, of course, this is what gardening is all about.

part i
SOWING

GARDEN
PREPARATION

You've been sitting indoors, dreamily browsing through garden catalogs during long winter evenings, and can hardly wait to start digging and planting a garden. Spring is the natural time to translate these dreams into reality, but fall is actually the best season to prepare a garden bed. Autumn preparation lets the snow and storms of winter break up clods and soak applied nutrients into the soil. But because most beginning gardeners get their first itch for a garden in the spring, we'll assume you will start just as soon as a handful of soil, squeezed in your hand, doesn't remain in a hard ball when you open your hand.

A family of four can easily use a vegetable plot 10 by 16 feet, which can yield a variety of vegetables from late spring until fall with about two hours of work each week after the initial preparation and planting. But of course there is no average family or average yard, so you will have to stake out your first garden according to space available, the size of your family, and sun. In order to take advantage of sunny spots, you may have to use more than one site for your vegetables instead of a single contiguous plot.

Select a well-drained, sunny location with at least six hours of sun per day, preferably eight. A southeastern exposure gets the most sun and is frost-free earlier in the spring and later in the fall. Selecting the site and preparing the soil are the most important preliminaries to good garden culture, so no shortcuts are allowed!

To begin with, you'll need a spade to turn over and break up the soil; a steel rake to remove debris and smooth the surface; a cultivating hoe to remove weeds; a determination to stick with your project; and a strong constitution. Some limbering-up exercises done for a few weeks before spring-planting will prevent aching muscles and sore backs.

On the site (or sites) you have selected for vegetable plantings, dig down about twelve inches, turning over each shovelful of soil. Remove all lumps of sod (after shaking the dirt off), stones, and weeds. Then work the soil with your rake into a granulated texture along with the organic nutrients (i.e., nonchemical fertilizers) you are adding to the soil. Aged manure—cow, chicken, or horse—is ideal, so add it if you have access to any. We use pigeon manure, which doesn't need aging; but when that is unavailable, we apply a commercial organic fertilizer available at most garden centers. An equal amount of wood ashes should be applied too; if you don't have a fireplace, beg, borrow, or steal from your friends who do. You should also add three to four inches of compost, but if this is your first garden, you may have to substitute sand or shredded leaves to improve the texture of the soil.

Ideally, lime should have been put on the garden in late February or early March so the snow and rain can work it into the soil gradually. Lime "sweetens" the soil— that is, it makes acid soil alkaline. The term *pH*, which describes the acid or alkaline quality of any substance on a scale running from 0 to 14, is included in gardening nomenclature. Most vegetables and herbs need a slightly acid soil, 6 to 7 on the pH scale. You can determine the acidity or alkalinity of your soil and how much of the three basic nutrients it contains by testing it with a purchased kit or by mailing a sample to your local Agricultural Agent (check your local telephone book for the address) or the U.S. Department of Agriculture, Washington, D.C. 20250. Knowing the pH factor of your soil may sound terribly technical, but it is as important to gardening success as the temperature of your oven is to cooking success.

Just about everybody has soil problems, so don't worry; they can be corrected even if you're not a chemistry expert. The main nutrients needed are nitrogen, phosphorus, and potassium (sometimes called potash). You may have wondered what the numbers on bags of fertilizer mean: they refer to the percentage of these three nutrients in alphabetical order. For example, 5–10–5 means 5% nitrogen, 10% phosphorus, and 5% potassium. A 5–10–5 organic mix is a well-balanced fertilizer, and is probably the best to use for your first garden.

Vegetables need all three nutrients, but because each nutrient stimulates different parts of a plant, an additional application or one or more can be beneficial. Nitrogen promotes vigorous stem growth; phosphorus, fruit; potassium, roots. Above-the-ground crops such as lettuce, tomatoes, and peppers need nitrogen, which is found in organic fertilizers such as soybean meal, bonemeal, cottonseed meal, and dried blood. Bonemeal, dried blood, humus, and other organic materials encourage healthy fruit production by supplying phosphorus. Root vegetables such as beets, carrots, and onions benefit from potassium, derived from compost, wood ashes, and cocoashell residue.

A healthy beet crop is a good indication that the soil

is properly balanced for growing most other vegetables, so if either your beet tops or roots fail or do poorly you'll know your ground lacks one or more nutrients or that its pH is wrong. Definitely make a soil test and correct the problem condition(s).

Many gardeners, especially those who live in newly developed areas where the natural topsoil has been bulldozed away by careless builders, have a long struggle with heavy clay earth. This can be changed with patience and perseverance. Mixtures of sand, sifted coal ashes, manure, compost, and other organic matter applied over a period of years will produce a well-textured, friable soil. Meanwhile, remember that you should never attempt to work with clay soil when it is soaking wet.

A compost heap is indispensable to successful gardening because it adds a combination of nutrients and texturizers. After a few years of adding compost, you'll discover that your garden is fertile and almost pest-free. Healthy gardens actually repel enemies, because enemies ordinarily attack weak growth. It's well worth the effort to keep a compost heap all year, even though decomposition is minuscule in cold weather.

You can start a compost heap in May. Select a secluded location, with two to four hours of sun a day, close to the main garden, and hidden, if possible, from your neighbors—sometimes they become a bit peculiar about things they don't understand! The size depends on your needs: for a 10- by 16-foot garden, a 3- by 3- by 3-foot pile should more than suffice. The heap must be enclosed, otherwise it will be unsightly. Any number of materials can be used to build the enclosure—wire mesh, wood slats loosely joined together, or cinder blocks. Air should be able to circulate from the top to the bottom of the pile and on all four sides.

The basic ingredients for composting are layers of

dry leaves, preferably shredded, grass clippings (but be sure no weed killer has been used on the lawns they come from), a thin layer of topsoil now and then, natural fertilizers, healthy garden stalks and other leavings, wood ashes, lime, uncooked fruit and vegetable rinds and parings, coffee grounds, tea leaves, and cleaned egg and seafood shells. Don't add meat, bread, or anything else that might attract rodents or other animals. Wet the heap weekly if nature doesn't provide the rain, and keep the top concave to collect the water. Turn the pile with a pitchfork or shovel every ten to fourteen days to encourage decomposition.

In the fall there will be a rich, dark compost which should be spaded into the garden topsoil. Compost cannot be bought and you will have a great sense of satisfaction from having created your own.

Vegetables benefit from mulching, which keeps weed and pests to a minimum and the soil cool and moist during hot, dry weather, Biennials and perennials should be mulched in the fall if winter temperatures can drop below their survival levels. Good mulch materials are grass clippings, peat moss, straw, cottonseed hulls, peanut shells, pine needles, salt hay, cocoa beans, buckwheat hulls, sawdust, wood chips, shredded newspapers, and black-plastic sheets. Some of these are better adapted to one plant than another, so it's best to consult your garden center before buying: purchased mulches can be expensive. A three- or four-inch layer of mulch should be spread between garden rows, and about two inches around the plants themselves. Wood chips lend a rustic touch to garden paths.

When putting plants or seeds in the garden, be very careful to mark them either individually or with string stretched between little stakes. You'd be amazed at how easy it is to forget what you planted, and where. Very shortly, you can play two games called "Vegetable Watching" and "Hide-and-Go-Seek." Nature outsmarts me every year! Daily I check the results of my labor, occasionally finding a tiny cucumber, green pepper, or squash that has begun growth, but more often I find plants that have reached maturity and evaded me completely—bifocals and all! These games never stop delighting me.

Beware of droughts that often occur in late summer. A lack of rain and the scorching sun can cause considerable damage. Most vegetables require one to two inches of rain a week. To apply the equivalent of one inch of rainfall, you'll need two-thirds of a gallon of water for each square foot of soil. To measure the weekly rainfall, put a container in the garden to collect the rain and remember to consider evaporation when assessing the weekly accumulation.

On the other hand, summer downpours can be just as disastrous—especially to tall plants. Support them securely on poles, stakes, or broken tree branches so they can withstand wind and torrential rains. After a storm, prop up plants that have been knocked down or bent over.

An old proverb says that the best fertilizer for a plant is its owner's shadow. Scientific experiments suggest that a plant has emotions, so always remember that tender, loving care goes a long way—even with vegetables!

Four Sample Kitchen-Garden Plans

These samples are to help you plan your first vegetable garden. You and your family may have tastes very different from any combinations in these guides, but you can easily modify them after you have read the book.

First of all, notice that taller vegetables are placed at the rear of the garden, the lower-growing in front.

This is important because you don't want big tomatoes in August shading shorter peppers and cucumbers.

The plans indicate how garden space can be made more productive by using the same space for an early crop and a late crop. That is what the term *following* means; after harvesting a cool crop such as snow peas, you can use that space in the garden for setting out tomatoes (either purchased plants or plants you have raised from seed).

Staggering plants is another way to save space. You can fit five tomato plants in a 3- by 10-foot row, if you put three in the first row, and stagger two diagonally across from the three in the second row.

You probably won't be entirely satisfied with the results of your first garden plan, but that will make you all the more eager to start on your second-year plan!

SAMPLE GARDEN #1

13' x 13'

2 rows of snow peas followed by 1 row of tomatoes interplanted with basil	3'
2 rows of Bibb lettuce followed by 1 row of green peppers interplanted with 2 tarragon plants	2'
1 row of spinach followed by 1 row of yellow bush beans	2'
2 rows of beets followed by 3 hills of cucumbers	4'
4 rows of carrots and radishes, sown together	2'

SAMPLE GARDEN #2

13' x 13'

2 rows of shelling peas followed by 2 rows of pole limas spaced alternately with 2 thyme plants at either end	3'
1 row of cabbage interplanted with rosemary	2'
1 row of large onions	1½'
4 rows of loose-leaf lettuce (successive plantings) followed by 3 hills of summer squash	4'
1 row of head lettuce	1'
2 rows of garden cress followed by 1 row of cherry (dwarf) tomatoes	1½'

SAMPLE GARDEN #3

10′ x 16′

2 rows of climbing dwarf peas followed by 5 tomato plants spaced alternately	3′
1 row of parsley	1′
1 row of carrots and Bibb lettuce, sown together	1′
½ row of chives and ½ row of scallions	1′
1 row of beets followed by 1 row of green peppers	2′
4 hills of winter squash	4′
4 rows of radishes (successive plantings) followed by 1 row of green beans	2′
2 rows of garden cress followed by 1 row of bush limas	2′

SAMPLE GARDEN #4

10′ x 16′

2 rows of climbing (pole) limas trained on a fence	2′
1 row of spinach followed by 1 row of yellow beans	1½′
1 row of cabbage interplanted with marjoram	2½′
1 row of radishes and dill sown together	1′
1 row of beets followed by 2 rows of cherry (dwarf) tomatoes	2′
½ row of scallions and ½ row of leeks	2′
4 hills of summer squash	4′
1 row of carrots and Bibb lettuce, sown together	1′

COMPANION
PLANTING

Companion planting is a relatively new organic-gardening concept which is still being studied. Why certain plants are compatible with some and not with others is not entirely understood—perhaps, like people, they have inbred affinities or aversions that will never be completely explained.

The purpose of companion planting is to produce healthy, untainted vegetables without the use of chemical pesticides. Loyal organic gardeners are convinced of the value of harmonious planting, so do humor your vegetables with other growing friends before you devour them!

You can devise your own companion plantings by referring to the guide on page 29. Although far from complete, it is a guide with which you can experiment, and it offers suggestions for all the vegetables discussed in this book. Aromatic plants, both flowers and vegetables, attract and repel certain insects by their odor. Some plants protect others by luring pests away from their neighbors without harm to themselves. Others produce substances that are natural insect and disease repellents. For example, chives protect lettuce from aphids, and garlic repels mice, moles, Japanese beetles, and aphids. Marigolds scattered through the garden discourage nematodes and other pests. Rosemary deters Mexican bean beetles and cabbage-moth larvae; thyme discourages cabbage worms; tomatoes control asparagus beetles; and basil repels mosquitoes and flies. Although not exactly organic, almost empty beer cans placed horizontally in the garden lure slugs that usually emerge en masse after a rainstorm, crawl inside, become inebriated, and drown in a stupor. Dried blood, available at hardware stores, can be sprinkled around tender crops to discourage attacks from a variety of roaming animals.

A good natural spray can be made from a large onion chopped and pureed in a blender of water. Strain through cheesecloth into a spray jar. Or grind together 4 hot peppers, 4 onions, and 2 garlic bulbs. Add water to cover an inch above the mash ingredients. After marinating the mixture twenty-four hours, strain it through cheesecloth and add enough water to make a gallon. These easily made mixes are effective against many bugs, and are much less expensive and damaging than pesticides made from chemicals.

Many organic experts encourage the purchase of "good bugs" such as ladybugs and praying mantises, for they eat the "bad bugs." For example, a ladybug can eat about 50 aphids a day. She also relishes scale insects, mealybugs, and mites. We bought a few hundred of these pretty red bugs with their black spots, but soon they flew away, as the song says, and we hope our neighbors benefited. Praying mantises, on the other hand, take care of insects ladybugs don't like. The mantis is large and grotesque, generally colored brown or green. In spite of his ugliness, it is unlawful in many states to harm this hero of the garden world.

COMPANION-PLANTING CHART

Vegetables

Beans (bush)	like cucumbers	dislike onions
Beans (lima)	like corn	dislike beets
Beets	like onions	dislike pole beans
Cabbage	likes aromatic plants, potatoes, celery, dill, beets, onions, sage, rosemary	dislikes tomatoes
Carrots	like leaf lettuce, chives, rosemary, sage, tomatoes	dislike dill and aromatic herbs
Cucumbers	like beans and radishes	dislike potatoes and aromatic herbs
Lettuce	likes carrots, radishes, cucumbers	
Onions	like beets	dislike peas and beans
Peas	like carrots, radishes, cucumbers, beans	dislike onions and garlic
Radishes	like nasturtiums, cucumbers, lettuce	
Scallions	like beets, tomatoes, lettuce	dislike peas, beans
Spinach	likes strawberries	
Squash	likes nasturtiums	
Sweet peppers	like everything, especially marigolds	
Tomatoes	like chives, onions, parsley, marigolds, nasturtiums, carrots	dislike potatoes and cabbage

Herbs

Basil	likes tomatoes	dislikes rue
Chives	like carrots	
Dill	likes cabbage	dislikes carrots
Garden cress	likes carrots, radishes	
Marjoram	place throughout the garden	
Parsley	likes tomatoes	
Rosemary	likes cabbage and beans	
Tarragon	place throughout the garden	
Thyme	place throughout the garden	

STARTING SEEDS
INDOORS

If you enjoy a challenge, try starting seeds indoors. Once you master the techniques of proper temperature, humidity, and general growing conditions, you will find indoor gardening a fascinating prelude to spring.

New gardeners who don't want to risk unfavorable results should begin with some of the less fussy plants, such as garden cress and marigolds, and gradually include those which require more patience and knowledge, such as head lettuce, cabbage, tomatoes, peppers, and onions. Unless you live in a climate suitable for growing vegetables year round, these must all be started indoors or purchased as established plants.

Reputable firms stock fresh seeds (and of course you can order from those catalogs you've been perusing). Before you buy, look at the growing instructions and seed expiration dates, and try to select disease- and insect-resistant varieties. Some vegetables produce seed which can be used the following year, but many cross-pollinate, resulting in some undesirable characteristics. If you have ever seen a pumpkin that cross-pollinated with a melon, you know it can and does happen.

There are numerous containers in which to start your seeds. Clay, plastic, or peat pots are the most obvious, but how about cake tins or wooden boxes? Cardboard egg containers are ideal—just wrap the bottoms with aluminum foil to collect any water seepage and cover with the tops. Seeds should be sown in equal parts of sphagnum, peat moss, perlite, and vermiculite, a mixture you can concoct or buy.

Six to ten weeks before the last expected frost date in your area, place three to six seeds in a container (depending on its size), sprinkle well with water but do not drench, cover with newspaper, cardboard, aluminum foil, or plastic, and keep in a dark, warm place (70°) until seedlings appear. It's essential to keep the soil moist during this period. Germination varies from four to ten days, depending on the variety. The minute sprouts appear, uncover and move into filtered, not strong, light.

When the first "true" leaves appear (sooner if the sprouts seem too crowded), remove two of the weaker seedlings and place the strongest plant(s) in a draftless, warm, humid room with six hours of direct sun. The container must be rotated daily to achieve a proper balance of sunlight on all sides and kept moist by very gentle sprinkling. Watering is necessary when the potting material becomes dry an eighth of an inch below the surface.

When seedlings develop about four leaves, they must be transplanted into larger living quarters without damage to the roots. Using a dibble, fork, or small stick, lift the baby seedlings carefully and plant one to two inches apart in a cold frame until it is time for them to go into the outdoor garden. This is called *hardening*, and means preparing plants to withstand conditions such as chilling, drying winds, high temperatures, and water shortages. You will have to experiment, but remember that you must keep these fragile plants warm and moist as you ever so

SPRING HARD-FROST DATE MAP

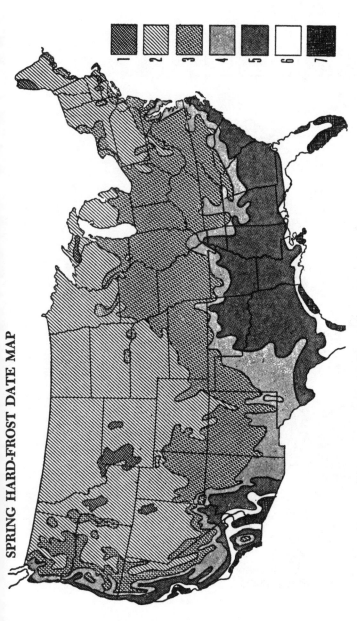

Average date of last expected spring frosts: Zone 1, June; zone 2, May 10–30; zone 3, April 10 to May 10; zone 4, March 20 to April 10; zone 5, February 28 to March 10; zone 6, February 8–28; zone 7, January 30 to February 8.

Map courtesy of Rodale Press, Inc., Emmaus, Pennsylvania

FALL HARD-FROST DATE MAP

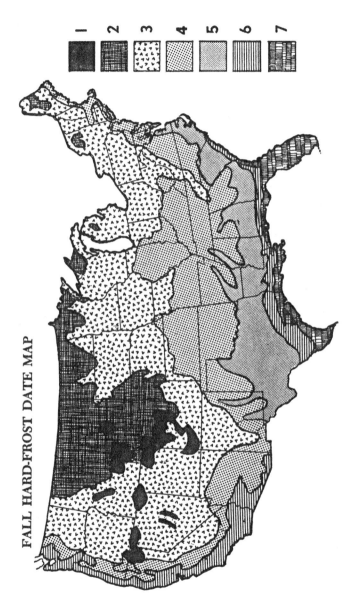

1–Aug. 30; 2–Sept. 10–20; 3–Sept. 30, Oct. 10; 4–Oct. 20–30; 5–Oct. 30, Nov. 10; 6–Nov. 20, Dec. 10; 7–Dec. 10–20. Dates given here are subject to local conditions and weather cycles.

Map courtesy of Rodale Press, Inc., Emmaus, Pennsylvania

gradually expose them to lower temperatures and less water. The soil should never become parched.

Once in the cold frame, there's no hurry to plant tomatoes, peppers, and other tender plants in the garden until the ground is warm and all danger of cold, wet weather has passed. An old Indian custom was to put tender plants into the ground the time the oak leaves burst into growth. If you don't have an oak tree, transplant about three weeks after the last frost-free date. "Cool," hardy plants such as lettuce, cabbage, and onions can withstand early outdoor planting and will even tolerate a light frost. Cabbage, spinach, and lettuce seeds can be sown directly into the cold frame if temperatures inside range between 40° and 50°. Not all seedlings necessarily survive so start more seeds than you need and encourage neighbors and friends to plant any extras.

For easy accessibility, good cold-frame dimensions are 6 feet long by 3 feet wide. Frames are usually deeper at the back, sloping toward the front so more sun reaches the plants. Sides constructed of redwood or other weathered lumber remain durable for many years. A clear plastic or glass cover that fits securely over the top protects the plants during cold weather. We have found that a cold frame built to use an old storm door as the cover is an ideal unit. It should have a southern exposure and be protected on all sides, if possible, from winter winds. In mild weather, open the top for gradually longer periods during the warm part of the day. When a cold spell comes, a warm covering should be placed around the enclosure at night. It's not a bad idea to keep a thermometer in cold frames because temperatures can fluctuate wildly.

Fill the cold frame with equal parts of sand, soil, and compost or well-rotted manure, leaving enough headroom for the plants to grow and not be crowded when the cover is closed. I always add a little bonemeal, and fertilize weekly with used tea leaves before sprinkling with tepid water.

Cold frames are good places to store winter vegetables, and can also prolong the growing season when young growth in the fall garden is moved into them.

Transplanting from the cold frame to the garden is relatively easy once you understand the system. Make a hole about the depth and width of a trowel and fill with water, allowing it to seep down before placing the plant into the hole. Transplant as much original soil around the roots of the plant as possible and set the plant at the same depth as in the cold frame. The roots should spread out and extend downward. Bring some of the moistened soil from the sides of the hole and pack it gently around the roots with your hand, rather than your trowel, as they should not be even slightly damaged or broken. Now fill the hole with the soil that you dug to make it, leaving the surface a little lower than the level of the surrounding ground. Fill this indentation with water and let it stand for an hour or so. Then press the remaining soil firmly around the plant.

If transplanting is done before the weather gets hot, and in the evening or on a cloudy day, you won't have to protect the small plants with baskets or other shade. But you will if there is a chance that hot sun will topple them over and kill them. Keep transplants well watered for two weeks to ensure a proper start.

CONTAINER
GARDENING

Miniature vegetable gardens are a year-round adventure and are becoming increasingly popular. Why not be the first in your neighborhood to grow vegetables in containers? It's an easy and pleasurable way to garden if you live in an apartment, town house, or condominium. A sunny balcony, patio, courtyard, porch, doorway, or windowsill can reap the treasures of a garden.

Containers may be almost anything that suits your fancy: plastic or clay pots, window boxes (redwood is extremely durable), tubs, old pails, bushel or wire baskets, barrels, or old drawers. Imaginative gardeners improvise with all sorts and conditions of materials, depending on what vegetables they want to raise and what they have on hand.

Cucumbers, green peppers, and tomatoes need five-gallon containers (dwarf tomatoes do well in two-gallon). Radishes, lettuce, scallions, spinach, cress, parsley, carrots, chives, and other herbs flourish in smaller containers that are about six inches deep and about six inches wide. For the complete culture of each vegetable, read the section devoted to it.

Perforate the base of any container so excess water can drain off. If a wooden container is used, it should be treated with a preservative. All containers must be washed throughly before planting.

Garden soil, particularly if you live in a high-rise apartment, can be a weighty problem. A purchased mixture of peat moss, sand, and fertilizer is available at hardware stores and garden centers, and is much easier to transport and less taxing on floor and balcony supports. But whether you use soil or a mix, first put an inch of gravel in the bottom of the container for drainage and then follow the general instructions for planting. You almost never need to weed plants in pots, but they do need to be watered more frequently. The soil should be moist to the touch, but never soggy: too much water rots the roots.

Leafy vegetables such as lettuce and cabbage can stand more shade than root vegetables (radishes, carrots, beets). Root vegetables however, need less sun than cucumber, peppers, and tomatoes, which need warmth and full sun. In other words, plant the latter where they will receive the most sun, and your leafy and root vegetables in more shaded areas, such as under the leaves of the peppers and tomatoes.

Tomato, pepper, and cabbage plants are especially recommended to the beginner, but many companies are offering other vegetables specifically designed for container gardening, such as Short 'n Sweet carrots and Tom Thumb and Salad Bowl lettuce. Cucumbers, beans, and tomatoes can be trained on a trellis to save space and look more ornamental. Many herbs adapt very well to container gardening.

Small sowings of different vegetables every three or four weeks during the growing season can furnish you with a surprising amount of produce. When the weather turns cold, expose herbs to gradually warmer temperatures on a porch or in the garage before bringing them into the house, where they can be placed in a sunny window to be enjoyed indefinitely. Unless you have a cold frame, greenhouse, or a perfect combination of heat, sunshine, and humidity, most vegetables do not perform well indoors.

part ii
REAPING

BEANS

Someone once said, "A garden is not a garden unless it has some beans growing." There are more than five hundred varieties of beans. For a small garden, select a disease-resistant bush or climbing variety—either green or yellow (wax). Tendercrop or Burpee's Brittle Wax are both excellent. Of the two types, the yellow snaps are considered more of a delicacy both in flavor and because they perish quickly and so are often unavailable on most produce counters. Growing beans is virtually foolproof. The most laborious chore is harvesting continuous and abundant yields.

The soil for all members of the legume family should be well drained and reasonably fertile, but it should not contain too much nitrogen. Mixtures of sand, peat moss, and sifted wood ashes provide phosphorus and potassium and loosen crusty, hardpan soil that makes it difficult for the seeds to sprout. Plant all bean varieties in ground that is thoroughly warm, otherwise seeds will stay dormant and possibly rot. Beans are among the last vegetables that should be planted in your garden. Many garden books stress the danger of growing beans in a low, soggy area,

SNAP BEANS

but our experience belies this theory. We've had fantastically prolific yields of both yellow and green bush beans from a warm, *damp* part of our garden.

Soak bean seeds in lukewarm water overnight and plant, eye down, one and a half inches deep in friable soil—or only an inch deep if the soil is heavy. Seeds should be spaced about six inches apart in rows fourteen inches apart. These dimensions are approximate: do follow the instructions on the seed packet. Make consecutive sowings every ten days until midsummer. Harvesting begins in about sixty days.

Careful cultivation of beans is necessary because of their shallow root system. Unlike most other vegetables, weeding, cultivation, harvesting—even walking between the rows—should be avoided when plants are wet with dew or rain, because it is then that the spores of bean canker can be spread. Canker can destroy an entire crop. I have been guilty of offending all of these rules with no ill effects, but would feel guilty if I did not alert you to potential danger. Purchasing disease-resistant seeds and planting them in an organic garden, however, should give healthy crops.

Pick beans when the seeds inside are too small to give the pod an uneven outline—or when the bean is about one-quarter inch in diameter. This is the peak period of tenderness and flavor. Picking encourages continued crop production.

Benefit from the A, B, and C vitamins beans provide by cooking immediately after harvesting until just tender. Canning, freezing, or drying any surplus provides treats all through the winter.

To freeze, wash and remove stems and injured spots. Cut to desired specifications or leave whole. Cover with boiling water and boil for 3½ minutes. Drain and immediately immerse in ice water until cool. Drain again and pack into plastic freezer bags or boxes available at hardware stores.

Almond Green Beans in Brown Butter

10 ounces frozen green beans
¼ cup slivered, blanched almonds
¼ teaspoon salt
2 teaspoons fresh lemon juice
½ cup butter

Put frozen beans in boiling salted water and cook until tender. Drain and add the butter, which has been heated and stirred constantly until brown without burning. Gently stir in remaining ingredients. Makes four small servings.

Lima Beans

Although pole limas are generally believed to be more delicious and heavier yielders, they are slower growers than bush limas. Depending on your location, the pole-lima pods may not develop fully before a frost, and low temperatures are damaging. Pole limas need three to four months of summer temperatures, so start them indoors four weeks before the outdoor planting date by placing them, eye down, in peat pots and keeping them moist in a sunny window. If pole limas are one of your favorite vegetables, it's worth the extra effort to start them early, and, of course, pole limas save precious garden space. Kentucky Wonder is a fast-growing pole bean with a tender, meaty flavor, and it freezes well.

Eight-foot-high poles spread four feet apart, connected horizontally and diagonally with heavy twine or wire, will support the long vines, or the vines may be

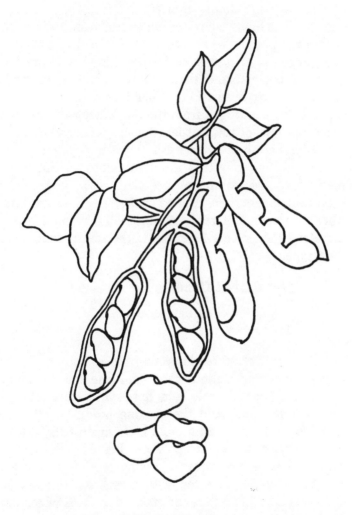

LIMA BEANS

trained to grow on a wire or fence. Lightly tie the growing vines to the support you have selected.

Seeds should be planted four inches apart, and twice as deep as their circumference.

Harvest limas when the bean seed can just be seen within the pod, or when your sixth sense thinks they are ripe. Fordhook No. 242 or Burpee's Improved are both excellent choices, and their culture is the same as for green and wax beans. Like other legumes, beans obtain much of their nitrogen from the air, leaving the soil with more, not less, of this nutrient for crops next year.

Limas are best eaten fresh, but can be dried, frozen, or canned. Any way they are a substantial addition to a meal. For some reason—my peculiar taste, I guess—I like succotash made from canned rather than frozen limas. There are many different canning methods, but I'm passing along the process I believe is the safest, easiest, and least expensive.

Hot-Packed Canning for Lima Beans

1 quart shelled lima beans
1 teaspoon salt

Shell and clean tender young limas. Drop them into a pan of boiling, salted water and boil for 5 minutes. Spoon the beans loosely into hot, sterilized, unchipped pint or quart jars. Add the cooking liquid to within an inch below the lid. Tap a table knife against the sides of the jar to eliminate air pockets. Immediately seal by firmly screwing the caps. Wipe any residue off the jars.

Use a large pot fitted with a rack to keep the jars from touching the bottom or each other. This water bath completes the canning process. The pot must be large enough so that the tops of the jars are covered by at least an inch of water throughout the cooking process. Slowly immerse the rack with the sealed jars into steaming, but not boiling water. Cover and bring to a vigorous boil. Uncover and keep boiling for three hours. Cool and store.

Succulent Succotash

1 16-ounce jar canned limas
1 16-ounce package frozen or canned corn
1½ cups heavy cream
½ teaspoon ground black pepper
salt to taste

Drain and mix vegetables together in the top of a double boiler (reserve liquid for soup or stew). Stir in remaining ingredients and heat until hot. Serves 10–12.

BEETS

Beets are double-dividend vegetables that provide tender above-the-ground greens and delicious beneath-the-ground roots. They are an asset to any salad and a splendid hot dish. Many gardeners raise a mild-flavored crop of beet greens instead of stronger-flavored spinach. Most beet-seed varieties are easy to grow anywhere. They mature quickly (in approximately fifty days), so you can make as many as three successive sowings two months apart, except in the extreme north, where winter arrives early.

Because beets prefer cool weather, your first crop will probably be the healthiest. As the weather becomes warmer, beets become more susceptible to pests such as flea beetles. If you find them nibbling at the leaves, spray with an organic solution (see page 28).

Sow the seeds an inch deep and two and one-half inches apart, as early as the soil can be worked, in rows twenty inches apart in a deeply prepared bed of loam and sand. Root vegetables, more than others, dislike crusty, heavy-clay soil.

The green tops can be harvested when they are six

BEETS

inches high; the root may be allowed to grow anywhere from the size of a marble to that of a golf ball. If you have planted the seeds too closely and find it necessary to thin the rows, the young, tender tops can be added to a salad, or the entire plant can be transplanted. Mulching encourages verdant growth after the row has been cultivated.

Early Wonder, Crosby's Egyptian, and Detroit Dark Red, all standard varieties, are suitable for early planting. Beets provide vitamins A and C, riboflavin, and folic acid. They can be harvested after frost and stored for the winter in a cool place by interspersing them in a box, basket, or galvanized can with slightly moist sand.

This two-in-one vegetable combination is usually served hot, but if roots are cooked, slivered, and cooled, or the green tops washed and crisped, they make a pleasant addition to any salad.

When using sand-stored beets, wash and cook until tender. Save the liquid. Remove the skins and try this recipe.

Chinese Pickled Beets

1 pound small beets (if large, slice)
⅓ cup sugar
⅓ cup vinegar
2 teaspoons cornstarch
8 whole cloves
1 tablespoon vegetable oil
½ teaspoon vanilla
1 tablespoon ketchup
½ cup beet juice
salt to taste
dash of pepper

Mix sugar and cornstarch well in shallow pan. Add vinegar, cloves, salt, pepper, oil, and vanilla. Blend well. Add beets and beet juice and cook over medium heat, stirring constantly until thickened (3–5 minutes). Serves 4.

CABBAGE

"Oh, thrice and four times happy those who plant cabbage," wrote Rabelais in 1545. Cabbage is a versatile favorite, and is reported to have been around for two thousand years.

Don't make the mistake of overplanting. An ounce of seeds will produce up to 2,500 plants—a bit much for a home garden unless you have a vegetable stand, or are prepared to make oceans of sauerkraut!

Early-summer cabbage is easier to raise if it is started indoors or purchased as an established plant. Sowing seeds directly into the ground is not advisable in climates where the summer season is short. Start indoors in March by covering seed with a half-inch of soil (see page 32). Transfer seedlings into the cold frame about the time the fourth, "true" leaf appears, planting two inches apart, and gradually harden until a few weeks before the last heavy frost. Then transfer to the outdoor garden. Depending on the variety—large or small heads—the rows should be spaced two to three feet apart with fourteen to eighteen inches between each plant. Late-summer plantings

CABBAGE

require more space than those planted in the spring. If seeds are sown directly into the outdoor garden, leave seven inches between each until plants are six to eight inches high, and then thin according to the foregoing instructions.

Plants should be set deeply in a well-drained, well-textured soil that has been dressed with some bonemeal. Water and firm the soil before scattering a final touch of fertilizer and wood ashes around the individual plants. Do not plant cabbage in the same bed cabbages were grown the previous year.

To ward off cutworms, encircle the plant with a cardboard collar extending one inch into the ground and one and one-half inches above the ground. Marigolds and white geraniums in the cabbage patch are good pest repellents. If enemies still attack, spray with an organic solution (see page 28).

When the plants mature and become top-heavy, "hill" them by heaping additional soil around the stalks to keep them from toppling over. Harvesting occurs from sixty-five to one hundred twenty-five days after planting and is determined by a well-formed, round, hard head. If it feels rubbery, it's not quite ready.

Ruby Ball, obviously a red, not green, cabbage, is easily and quickly grown and, after the head is formed, can be left in the ground for a month without bursting or bolting. Savoy, a green variety, is fine-flavored and longer-growing—excellent for salads and cooking—and thrives on spring, summer and fall plantings.

Omit supplemental feedings on late crops. Cabbage is a hardy vegetable and can withstand a couple of light frosts without damage. When it really gets cold, cover with plastic or about a foot of mulch and leave in the garden until severe weather sets in. At that point, store the heads upside down in a dry area at a temperature hovering around 35° (first removing all injured outer leaves). Wrapped in newspapers, cabbage will stay fresh for at least three months or until you have a hankering for a tangy dish of coleslaw full of vitamins A, C, and K. Cabbage is delicious cooked and served with corned beef—a traditional New England dinner.

Have you ever made your own sauerkraut? It's an easy but slow process, and you'll be pleased with a good, old-fashioned accomplishment—one that will make you proud to say, "I made this!"

Sauerkraut

5 pounds fully matured green cabbage
¼ cup salt

Wash, quarter, and thinly slice cabbage heads. Mix well with salt and let stand an hour to wilt slightly. Pack firmly in a large, nonmetallic crock and cover with a piece of clean white cloth. Anchor the top with a plate or heavy weight. This process is called *curing* and will take at least 2 weeks, probably longer. A scum will form, which must be removed daily. Replace the cloth frequently. Keep the crock at 85° if possible. The kraut is cured when scum no longer forms.

At this point, pack the kraut into 7 pint-size, sterilized jars and cover with juice from the crock, leaving ½ inch headroom. If there is not enough liquid, add hot brine made by boiling a tablespoon of salt and a pint of water. Seal the jars securely, according to the manufacturer's instructions, and put them into a kettle of cold water that is 2 inches above the top of the lids. Be sure the jars do not touch one another. Bring slowly to boil and cook for 30 minutes. Makes 7 pints.

Pork Chop Casserole

1 pound homemade sauerkraut
1 16-ounce can stewed tomatoes
1 small onion, diced
1 apple, peeled, cored, and diced
4 pork chops
salt to taste

Mix all ingredients together, except pork chops. Place in greased casserole. In separate pan, brown the chops on both sides, remove fat, and place them on top of the casserole mixture. Cover and bake in 350° oven 45 minutes. Remove the cover and bake 15 minutes longer. Serves 4.

CARROTS

The sunshine vegetable with its sweet flavor and crisp freshness needs a deeply prepared, friable, enriched bed to produce strong, unstunted carrots. Stones and clods in the soil cause poorly formed, forked roots. This vegetable tolerates some shade.

The tiny seeds may be sown outdoors in the spring as soon as the ground can be worked. A good planting method that saves time, space, and energy is to mix a package of carrot seeds with radish or lettuce seeds, and sow them together a quarter-inch deep if the soil is heavy, or a half-inch deep in light soil. Radishes or lettuce matures rapidly and thus identifies the row. Harvesting the earlier vegetable greatly reduces the need to weed, thin, and cultivate the carrots. Carrots should stand no less than three inches apart in rows six to eight inches apart. Add a mulch of coffee grounds and use any thinnings (both tops and roots) to garnish salads. If you don't like them, add them to the compost collection.

Plant successive crops every two weeks until midsummer. Certain varieties such as Danvers and Bonus Spartan are ready in seventy-five days and are excellent for both salads and cooking. Royal Chantenay, an outstanding favorite, matures in seventy days and can be

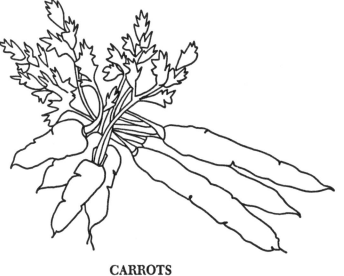

CARROTS

planted throughout the growing season. Harvest carrots when they're one half to one inch in diameter and have optimum flavor. Often the top of the root can be seen protruding just slightly above the soil. Bushy and heavy top growth also signal harvest-time. If the soil is dry and hard from lack of rain, you might have to use a hand spade to get carrots out of the ground.

Carrots can be stored over the winter in a cool box of sand, or you may opt to let them stay in the garden by covering the plants with fifteen inches of leaves to protect them from frost and heavy snows.

Full of vitamins A, B, C, and K, carrots can be slivered into salads or served by themselves as sticks sprinkled with fresh dill. Soaking carrots in water destroys precious vitamins, so avoid curls unless you're willing to sacrifice some nourishment. Overcooking also diminishes both vitamins and flavor. Save the cooking liquid for soups, casseroles, pot roasts, etc. Carrots can also be canned and frozen. Not every vegetable has so many storage potentials. They are, indeed, a worthwhile investment.

Mint-Glazed Carrots

    6 medium-size fresh carrots, washed, peeled,
       and sliced lengthwise
    salt to taste
    2 tablespoons melted butter
    2 tablespoons brown sugar
    1 teaspoon lemon juice
    ½ cup fresh mint leaves

Cook carrots in boiling, salted water for 15 minutes or until crunchy-tender. Drain. Mix remaining ingredients together and pour over carrots. Glaze by tossing gently over low heat until liquid disappears. Remove the mint. Serves 2.

CUCUMBERS

There are several ways to grow cucumbers. To save space, train them on a trellis or fence and anchor the vines as they mature. The anchoring ties should not be thin string that can bite into the vines. Use purchased flat ties or strips of sheets or nylon hosiery.

The most popular method of planting is in eight-inch hills spaced four feet apart. This is an especially good method for spring planting because the raised mounds stay warm despite the occasional chilly day or night. Plant five seeds a half-inch deep in each hill. When the plants are an inch high, remove two, leaving the three strongest separated by a few inches so the vines will not choke one another. Instead of discarding healthy-looking thinnings, transplant them two feet apart in rows four feet apart.

Cucumbers require an exceedingly fertile, well-drained soil that has been carefully prepared by cultivating at least a foot below the hill and mixing a combination of compost, wood ashes, and fertilizer into it. Plant after the soil has become warm, and then five weeks later for a fall harvest.

Cucumbers, even in organic gardens, are subject to

CUCUMBERS

attack from the cucumber beetle. Interplanting with garlic, onions, and marigolds helps control this pest. Some authorities suggest planting a melon seed, or three radish seeds, along with the cucumber seeds to repel the beetles.

Cucumbers mature in about two months. Daily picking prolongs production. Most varieties are at their tasty, crunchy best when they're about five inches long. Left on the vine too long they become seedy and less meaty. To avoid injury to the mother plant, cut the fruit with a sharp knife and leave a small part of the stem on the vine.

Any hybrid, disease-resistant package of seed can yield a bounty crop of a hundred cucumbers. Victory, for example, has vigorous vines and resists many cucumber diseases. If you want to grow cucumbers for pickling, garden catalogs recommend small varieties suited to that purpose. Burpless, guaranteeing just that, has a gourmet quality with an unusual flavor, but it doesn't taste quite the same as a "true" cucumber.

Although some of the vitamins A, B, and C found in cucumber are lost this way, we like them thinly sliced (skins and all), marinated in vinegar, chilled, and then drained and served with a dab of sour cream and a touch of fresh dill.

Cucumbers may not be as popular as some other vegetables, but their cool, ice-green crispness epitomizes the joys of summer eating.

To preserve, select cucumbers that are about five inches long and proceed with the following.

Bread-and-Butter Pickles

2 quarts unpeeled, thinly sliced cucumbers
3 cups thinly sliced white onions
2½ tablespoons salt
2½ cups sugar

1½ cups vinegar
½ tablespoon mustard seed
½ tablespoon celery seed
¾ teaspoon turmeric

Place cucumbers in a bowl or crock and cover with salt. Leave in refrigerator overnight. Remove and rinse in cold water. Drain well. Add remaining ingredients. Bring to a boil. (Do not use copper utensils.) Pack cucumbers and liquid into hot, sterile pint jars, leaving ½ inch headspace. Seal glass (not metal) lids tightly. Process in boiling water for 5 minutes. Makes about 4 pints.

HERBS

Herbs are important to organic gardening because they help keep vegetables free from pests. They also require very little space, have unlimited culinary uses, and lend a nostalgic Williamsburg charm to any garden. Most of them need sandy, unenriched, well-drained soil in full sun. (Rich loams inhibit the production of oils, which create fragrance and flavor.)

As attractive as herbs look in formal beds, it is more practical to intersperse them as companion plantings in the vegetable garden. By now you must have wondered how herbs can be planted in rich soil! The answer is to plant them in two locations—one to benefit vegetables and the other to benefit you! Dill, for example, repels the green tomato worm when planted next to tomatoes. But the rich soil in the vegetable garden makes the dill virtually flavorless. So plant dill in two places—some for the tomatoes and some for you. On the other hand, chives can tolerate rich, vegetable-garden soil (and less sun); tarragon tolerates some shade; and garden cress needs rich soil.

A few short rows of your favorite herbs are ample, and you can pot your favorites at the end of the growing season and bring them inside for winter growth on a windowsill that gets six hours of sun a day or the equivalent under fluorescent lights.

Before planting herbs, consider whether they are biennials, perennials, or annuals, and their height at maturity. If you have space for an herb garden, the orderly cascading of their branches in planned sequence is most attractive.

Small amounts of fresh herbs used with discretion in soups, salads, vegetables, and casseroles and on meat, poultry, and fish can convert a mundane meal into a gourmet feast. If you have a bit of English or Chinese in your past, try concocting your own private blends of exotic herbal teas.

When herbs begin producing flowers, pinch the blossoms immediately so the plants will continue to leaf. The time to cut leaves for drying is generally just before the first flowers appear. Harvest just after the morning dew has evaporated. Hang sprigs upside down, fastened with rubber bands, in loose bunches, or spread them on a clean, porous surface such as mesh screen and store them in the shade, where cool, dry air can circulate through the leaves. Label each type because they look almost alike when they are dry. After they are thoroughly dry, the leaves must be removed from the stems (a tedious job) and stored in tightly sealed jars away from direct sunlight. Some herbs, such as basil, may be frozen if they are blanched for fifty-seconds, cooled, and wrapped in foil before storing in the freezer. Chefs beware—dried herbs are stronger than fresh ones; a teaspoon of dried herbs equals a tablespoon of fresh ones.

Annuals started from seed germinate readily as a rule, but perennials are slow to germinate because of thin, hard seed covering. They are best purchased as established plants or rooted cuttings. If you decide to experiment with perennial seeds, place them in the freezer, defrost, and repeat the procedure three times to soften the hard shell.

Basil

Common basil has either purple-tinged or solid-green leaves with white or purple flowers that are attractive in either a flower or vegetable bed. Seeds from any of the fifty varieties of this annual can be started indoors or planted directly into the outdoor garden when the soil has become warm. Allow two leaves to remain at the base of the plant after picking bunches for drying. New growth will appear in about a week, or other sowings can be made as late as mid-August.

Basil has a sweet, licorice flavor, more pronounced when the leaves are bruised or crushed. It is delicious in tomato dishes and in salads, and can be preserved by freezing, drying, or storing in olive oil or vinegar.

Kitchen sour flies go into seclusion if a few basil sprigs are nearby—and that beats using poisonous indoor sprays.

Chives

The perennial chive has hollow, dark-green leaves and can be started easily from seed or bulb. The bulbs are planted a half-inch deep—the seeds a quarter-inch deep —below a fertile soil. Firm the ground well after planting. Either full or partial sun is acceptable. Thin to stand in clumps of six little sprouts, nine inches apart both diagonally and horizontally. A healthy clump matures in about seventy days. Chives multiply rapidly and the bulbs must

BASIL

CHIVES

be divided every two or three years. If the flowers are not picked, the plant will bolt.

Snip the tops for a delicate onion flavoring in cottage cheese, salads, sour cream, and vegetables. Storage can be by chopping and freezing, or drying and storing. I prefer to pot them for indoor use. If placed in a sunny window, watered, and snipped often, they last indefinitely.

Dill

For a full, piquant crop of dill, sow a package of seeds in a ten-foot row, one-sixteenth to one-eighth inch deep, separated by twelve-inch rows, after the soil has become warm. When the seedlings are six or eight inches high, thin to stand twelve inches apart. Transplant the thinnings to the tomato patch. Seventy days later, or when it is two feet tall, the dill is mature. Successive sowings during late spring and early summer keep a fresh supply available as older plants go to seed.

The lacy branches are delicious garnishes on most salads, and delectable in potato salad. Some cooks find a light dill flavor enhances strong-flavored vegetables such as cooked cabbage or turnips, but the most common use, of course, is in making dill pickles. If this is your main reason for growing dill, wait until it reaches full maturity and forms yellow seeds. These should be dried before adding to the pickling liquid.

Garden Cress

Garden cress is similar to watercress, but unfortunately lacks the subtle flavor we associate with that brook-grown perennial. On the plus side, garden cress is the easiest and quickest garden vegetable to raise. This old English favorite bears an early-summer crop and is an

DILL

attractive garnish on meats, in salads, or with sandwiches of cream cheese and cucumber.

Sow seeds thickly, one-eighth inch deep in drills of rich soil divided by ten-inch rows, in earliest spring and at weekly intervals until mid-May. Once they are established, thin the plants to four inches apart. If sown too late in the season, cress quickly goes to seed and becomes bitter.

Seedlings appear in less than a week, grow rapidly, and may be harvested in three or four weeks by cutting with shears. It's possible to get several cuttings if the cropping is not too close. Upland and Winter Cress are biennials and need no winter protection. Harvest and enjoy this short-season vegetable while it lasts, because there is no way to store it.

Marjoram

Sweet marjoram, a cousin of wild marjoram (better known as oregano), is a perennial usually grown as an annual. In Greece it is called "joy of the mountains" and is planted on family graves so the departed can sleep in peace.

The tiny seed wants a sheltered home in rich, light soil that has been treated with lime, and it also enjoys a daily spray of warm water. If you pamper these pets, you'll be rewarded with an exotic aroma of leaves that are tasty in just about everything—stews, eggs, meat sauces, stuffing, salads, and soups. Marjoram also makes a delightfully sweet tea, and some people use it medicinally for colds and congestion.

Thin to ten inches apart in rows fifteen inches apart. Once it reaches maturity, usually in July, cut it back two or three inches to prevent blossoming. To cure for the winter, cut and dry just before flowering begins.

MARJORAM

Parsley

The two most common varieties of parsley are the curly-leaved "plain" and the more aromatic, darker-green, flat-leaved Italian. Both are biennials but can be raised as annuals. If you want the benefit of another year's growth, blanket parsley with twelve inches of leaves before frost sets in, and it will remain verdant for winter use. The following spring, remove flowers as soon as they appear so the plant will keep producing leaves. The second year's growth is a bit tougher and less flavorful, so if you're a parsley addict, by all means plant a new crop every year in ordinary soil containing compost, a little sand, and a touch of lime.

Before planting, soak the seeds overnight because they are extremely slow to germinate. Plant one-eighth inch deep in rows ten inches apart. Mixing parsley and radish seed is a good idea both to identify the row and to save space. Thin the parsley to six inches after harvesting the radishes. When the plants become bushy, harvest by snipping with scissors. If only a few sprigs are needed, use the outer ones.

Parsley is rich in vitamins A and C, a good source of iron, and probably has more nutritional value, ounce for ounce, than many of the dishes it garnishes! It is also an excellent natural pesticide, especially useful in the tomato garden.

To dry, place sprigs on a cooky sheet and bake in a 200° oven for an hour, or until dry. Discard the stems, put the leaves into jars that will seal tightly, and store in a dark cupboard.

To freeze, clip branches in the afternoon or when they are dry, place loosely in a plastic jar, and cover. Frozen parsley is too limp for garnishing, but it is excellent in soups and sauces. Parsley can also be potted and grown

PARSLEY

indoors in a sunny window. Water and snip frequently—
it becomes a little bitter if it is left unused for too long.

Rosemary

Resembling miniature pine trees, rosemary is a perennial, culinary evergreen that withstands zero temperatures.
It's one of the few herbs that grow in shrublike clumps of
three to six feet, and will run rampant if not kept trimmed.

Rosemary can be started from seed inside, but because of its size at maturity, most gardeners need only one
or two cuttings that root easily if planted three feet apart
in a light, dry, chalky soil that has been dressed with lime
and wood ashes. Winter mulch is needed if temperatures
drop below zero, or a plant can be potted and brought
indoors.

Culinary experts add a few dashes to salads, sauces,
soups, stews, and eggs, but its most special use is with
lamb and chicken roasts.

Tarragon (French)

Tarragon's most enchanting use is to convert an otherwise bland salad dressing into a taste treat. Soak branches
of this pungent herb in vinegar for ten days before using
the vinegar in a basic French- or Italian-dressing recipe.
Not many gardeners need enough tarragon to bother
growing it from seed, so use root cuttings or plants which
are generally available at garden or nursery centers.

Plant in light, well-drained soil with space for them
to grow about two feet wide and two feet high. They do
well in partial shade and will grow for many years if
mulched heavily to withstand temperatures below −10°.

Put a large branch of tarragon in the vinegar bottle,
and add small amounts of the fresh spring leaves to salads,

ROSEMARY

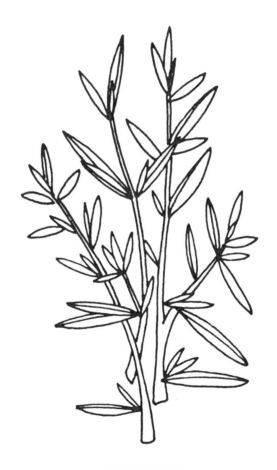

TARRAGON

chicken dishes, fish and shellfish dishes, chowders, and barbecue marinades. Tarragon is easily dried.

Thyme

From ancient times, thyme has been associated with courage, well-being, and happiness. Could there be a better herb to grace your garden than one associated with assets?

A perennial, similar to evergreens, thyme keeps its leaves all year and bears blossoms of many colors. Among the scores of species, common ("French") thyme is considered the best for cooking purposes. It is an erect, shrubby plant that grows easily from root cuttings to a height of eight to ten inches in ordinary, well-drained locations. Mature plants should stand twelve inches apart. It takes about two years for thyme grown from seed to reach a usable size.

When the plants bloom, cut off almost half the stem along with the flowers. Mulch plants in the fall before heavy snows can damage these low shrubs by settling in the center and breaking branches.

Thyme is dried in the same manner as other herbs, and is used primarily as a savory seasoning for soups, stews, tomatoes, and meat stuffings.

A Few Herbal Recipes

Individual preferences for herbs or combinations thereof are as personal as the perfume a woman selects. No one combination will please all tastes. The herbs used in the following recipes can be increased, decreased, or in some cases eliminated entirely. It's up to you—and this is one of the best parts of cooking with a kitchen garden that produces such a wide choice of yummy flavors.

THYME

Herb Croutons

2 slices well-buttered bread
2 teaspoons freshly chopped chives
½ teaspoon fresh thyme leaves

Mix chives and thyme and sprinkle over the buttered bread. Cut into cubes and broil until golden brown on both sides (about 2 minutes a side). Cool and store in tightly covered jar until ready to serve in soups or salads. (Recipe can easily be doubled or tripled.)

Herb Vinegar

2 tablespoons fresh tarragon
1 tablespoon fresh basil
1 tablespoon fresh dill
1 pint wine vinegar

Bruise the herbs with a wooden mallet and place in a nonmetallic bowl. Bring vinegar to boil and pour over the crushed herbs. Stir. Funnel mixture into the vinegar bottle. Seal tightly and store in a warm dark cupboard for 10 days, shaking daily. Then strain the mixture through cheesecloth until clear, return to the bottle, cap, and store in a dark, warm place until ready to use with a basic French- or Italian-dressing recipe.

Bouquet Garni

1 teaspoon dried marjoram leaves, crushed
½ teaspoon bay leaves, crushed
1 teaspoon dried parsley
1 teaspoon dried tarragon
1 teaspoon dried thyme
5-inch-square cheesecloth, double thickness
heavy-duty white thread or string

The easiest way to make a *bouquet garni* is to mix the herbs and put them in the center of the cheesecloth. Draw the 4 corners together and fasten with string to prevent the herbs from getting out of the cloth.

For an attractive hostess present, however, you might want to make a nicer container for the herbs by stitching loosely around the edges of the cheesecloth, gathering to form a bag, filling with the herb mixture, and sewing to close. Whatever method you use, leave a long thread hanging for easy removal.

Add a *bouquet garni* to stews or soups for 2 hours or longer, if that is what the recipe requires. Let the thread hang outside the kettle for easy removal. This size *bouquet garni* is sufficient for 4 quarts of liquid.

Chopped Chive Butter Balls

2 tablespoons soft butter
2 teaspoons chopped chives

Mix together, divide into two balls, and serve on top of opened baked potatoes. Serves 2.

LETTUCE

A garden started in the spring wouldn't be complete without lettuce, king of the salad crop. The two main types grown in small gardens are Bibb and leaf. The seeds may be sown every two weeks until late spring, and again one and one-half months before the first frost is predicted. Quickest and easiest to grow are the loose-leaf types such as Black-Seeded Simpson, Oak Leaf, or the ever popular Salad Bowl. They grow from seed to maturity in about forty-two days, but you can begin serving them much sooner. When the leaves are an inch high, it's thinning time—and you have the makings of your first salad.

Wait until temperatures reach 60° during the day before sowing leaf or Bibb directly into the garden. Sow sparingly, and when the leaves get crowded, thin to six inches apart in rows a foot apart. Germination may not occur if seeds are planted more than a quarter-inch deep.

Unlike head varieties, loose-leaf needs full sun and can be harvested by picking only a few leaves at a time, early in the day while still covered with dew. To keep it crisp after picking, wash it thoroughly in cold water,

BIBB LETTUCE

shake off excess moisture, and blot with paper towels until dry before storing it in a plastic bag or crisper in the refrigerator.

The most common lettuce found on produce counters is iceberg, a head type that is more difficult to raise than loose-leaf or Bibb, because it takes much longer to grow and doesn't always survive exposure to hot weather. It should be started indoors and transferred to the cold frame after four true leaves appear and temperatures are at least 28°. After hardening about six weeks, space a foot apart in the outside garden. The heads should flourish and be ready for harvesting in three months. Plants will withstand the heat better if in partial shade or protected by the leaves of other vegetables. Once they are established, a heavy mulch of about four inches keeps the ground moist and cool. Great Lakes is highly recommended as one of the best hot-weather survivors.

Bibb lettuce, a cross between the head and loose-leaf types, offers all the pluses of both and requires the same growing conditions as loose-leaf. Burpee's Bibb is slow to bolt (go to seed) and a good choice for the new gardener. Lettuce crops need a rich, cool organic bed, heavy with phosphorus. Attacks from cutworms and aphids can be controlled by putting heavy paper collars around the young plants and encircling them with wood ashes to prevent little bunnies and other animals from nibbling away at *your* salad. Romaine, escarole, and curly endive require similar but more exacting culture conditions and should be left to the seasoned gardener.

Lettuce is rich in vitamins A and C, and offers a big return on a small investment. Unfortunately, there is no long-term preservation method. Refrigerated, iceberg outlasts the more perishable loose-leaf types; and when it begins to wilt, it can be cooked and served as a mild and interesting hot dish.

Braised Lettuce

1 medium-size head iceberg lettuce, cut in 8 sections
1 tablespoon butter
garlic salt to taste
thyme to taste

Melt butter in covered pan. Add lettuce and seasonings and gently braise until soft. Serves 3.

ONIONS

At least one member of the pungent onion family belongs in your garden. Fall is the best time to prepare a bed for early-spring planting, which should be four to six weeks *before* your area's frost-free date. The most common onions are the large red, yellow, or white varieties; leeks; scallions, garlic and chives (see page 71). Gourmet cooks often use shallots, but they are difficult to raise and are mainly imported from Europe.

Onions are hardy cool-weather crops requiring a fine, well-textured soil enriched with about four inches of compost, ample moisture, and full sun. Green onions and leeks are the exceptions that can tolerate some shade. It takes up to four months for large onions to mature from seed, so onion sets or bulbs are generally recommended. They not only mature faster than seeds but are more resistant to disease. Plant the sets six inches apart in rows fifteen inches apart, twice as deep as the size of the bulb. If you intend to use some of the thinnings for salads, they may be spaced three inches apart, and thinned when growth is eight to ten inches high or about a hundred days after planting.

ONIONS

A thorough hoeing and weeding and the addition of fertilizer are essential once a month during the growing season, which can be extended until midsummer by planting bulbs every two weeks from early spring. One-quarter-inch mulching with grass clippings or broken straw helps the soil stay cool and moist. When the mulch begins to erode, repeat the application. Once the bulbs reach full size, stop watering and feeding.

Harvesting can begin when the leaves turn brown or topple over. You can speed this process by bending the stalks of every other plant to a prone position, thus allowing more light and air to penetrate the alternate bulbs. If you want to harvest all the onions at the same time, bend the stalks of every plant. Dig the bulbs in the morning before frost sets in. Dry for two weeks before eating, or store surplus in a box of sand in a cool place.

Creamed Onions

8 large white onions, peeled and quartered
½ pint heavy cream
salt to taste
paprika to taste
1 tablespoon flour

Boil onions in water for 20 minutes. Pour off liquid, add fresh water to cover, salt, and bring to a gentle boil until the onions fall apart. Drain off liquid; add cream, paprika, and flour to thicken. Make 1 day before serving. Reheat. Serves 6.

Leek

Leek has a milder flavor than large onions but is stronger than chives. The relatively long, slender stems and green leaves are chopped into tiny pieces and used primarily to season soups, meats, and salads. Plant the seeds one-quarter to one-half inch deep at least twenty inches from the nearest plantings. Scatter thinly in furrows and cover with light soil. Thin to four inches when five to six inches high. Harvesting takes place in about 130 days, or sooner if bulbs rather than seeds are used. The flavor is improved if soil is mounded up around each plant as it develops—this process is called *blanching*. When bulbs are about an inch in diameter, and the white growth is five or six inches long, they may be pulled. If not served fresh, they can be chopped and frozen in a tightly covered bowl.

Rich Leek Soup

10 leeks (roots only)
2 tablespoons chopped onion
4 cups chicken broth
3 large potatoes, diced
2 cups heavy cream
¼ cup butter
salt and pepper to taste
1 bay leaf
¼ teaspoon dried thyme

Wash and thinly slice white leek roots. Add onions and leek to melted butter and simmer until soft and light brown. Add chicken broth and diced potatoes. Mix well and add remaining seasonings. Boil gently until potatoes are cooked. Add cream and blend well. Remove bay leaf. Makes 6 cups.

Scallions

Scallions are also called bunching onions. The leaves and bulbs are usually used in salads. Plant seeds one-

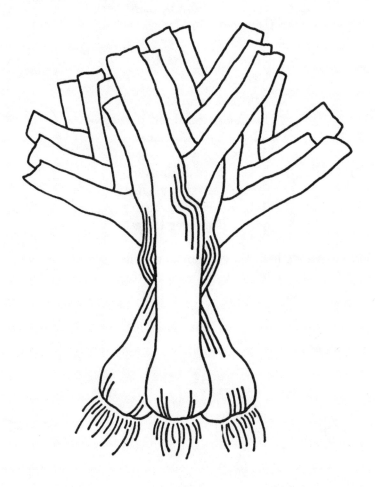

LEEKS

quarter inch deep and thin to two inches, leaving room for the bulbs to mature without touching. Full sun and blanching the shoots are necessary to form bulbs that mature in about four months. Harvest before frost, and either store in sand or hang in mesh bags in a cool, dark place out of the reach of rodents.

Green Goddess Dressing

12 scallions
2 green peppers
1 tablespoon dried parsley
12 anchovies, drained
1 garlic clove, crushed
1 cup French dressing
1 cup tart mayonnaise
1 tablespoon tarragon vinegar
salt and pepper to taste

Mince first 4 ingredients and mix. Add remaining ingredients, blend well, and chill overnight. Pour over mixed greens. Serves 12.

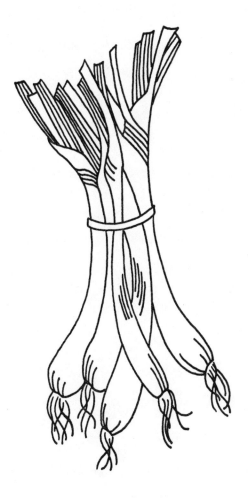

SCALLIONS

PEAS

When it comes to peas, sweet flavor and an early crop are major goals. They are a cool-season vegetable that needs planting just as soon as the soil becomes workable. Better still, prepare a rich, well-limed, sandy soil, laced with humus, in the fall. In Zone 4, we plant snow peas on St. Patrick's Day, and know some eager beavers who plant with great success in February.

Pea seeds will germinate when daytime temperatures are as low as 50°. Seed companies and some garden books encourage late-summer sowings—it's risky, however, because peas need considerable moisture and coolness that late-summer weather often does not provide. Many gardeners prefer to use garden space for more prolific yielders than peas. Late-winter and early-spring plantings will produce tender and succulent pods that can be eaten raw in a salad, or cooked, frozen, canned, or dried.

There are four varieties of peas: the English type that grows six feet; edible podded varieties known as snow or Chinese peas; sweet sugar dwarfs that are similar to snow peas, only larger and heavier; and peas grown

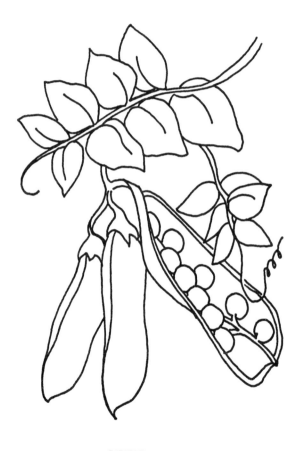

GREEN PEAS

for drying. The first three are most commonly raised by home gardeners. Peas contain vitamins A, B, C, and E.

We have a friend in Bucks County, Pennsylvania, who freezes and defrosts pea seeds three times before planting. Actually, you can prepare the hard shell for germination just as effectively by soaking the seeds overnight in lukewarm water before planting in shallow trenches, two to three inches deep and three inches apart. Successive sowings can be made at ten-day intervals until midspring.

For climbing varieties, construct a fence between the trenches by diagonally tying four to six lengths of string to heavy wooden stakes at each end of the row, and planting the seeds on either side of the fence. This system is a good space-saver. Bush peas are not recommended— they are more susceptible than the climbers to bug and bird attacks and require much more space.

It takes from fifty-five to sixty-eight days for peas to mature. Our favorite is Burpee's Sweet Pod, a snow pea ready to harvest in sixty-eight days or when the seeds are barely visible inside the shell. A highly tender and productive crop with edible pods, they're a delicacy not often available in stores, or costly when you're lucky enough to locate them.

Blue Bantam produces fifteen-inch vines bearing a heavy yield of shelling peas, and is highly recommended if you have the space. Popular dwarf peas are Alaska and Little Marvel, and are best picked when plump and firm—the more you pick, the greater the yield. A two-ounce package of any variety of seeds is needed for each person in the family.

If conditions are extremely hot, wet, or dry, plants will be damaged and the blossoms will fall. Unpredictable weather is always a challenge to those dependent on the elements, no matter what is planted, so get the peas in

SNOW PEA PODS

early and take a gamble—you'll probably come out a winner.

Once again, I like to do things the easy way by washing, blanching, cooling, and freezing. Snow peas should be blanched only a minute, but shelling peas require three minutes. Rather than lose the purity of snow peas (a staple in Chinese recipes), I opt for simplicity.

Snow Peas à l'Américaine

1 6-ounce package frozen garden snow peas
1 tablespoon butter
salt and pepper to taste

Place frozen peas into ½ cup boiling salted water. Return to a quick boil for a minute or two, or until peas are crunchy-tender. Drain, add butter and pepper. Serves 2.

PEPPERS

Sweet green-pepper plants add zest and glossy-green ornamental beauty to your garden. Thick foliage covers round, oblong, or bell-shaped fruits. Hot peppers may be raised in the same bed as sweet peppers.

It takes 110 to 120 days for the plants to produce their waxy fruit in a warm soil with full sun. In view of this, unless you live in a warm climate, it's advisable to start seeds indoors or purchase established plants such as Yola or California Wonder. It's even risky to start peppers indoors (six to ten weeks before transferring them into cold frames) unless you have soil temperatures controlled by electric coils.

Before planting the pepper plants, prepare the soil with a little lime, wood ash, and potash; and when the ground temperature reaches 70° to 80°, it is safe to plant them. Allow fourteen inches between the plants and two feet between the rows. Wood ashes sprinkled around every plant prevent enemies from attacking.

After the plants begin bearing, there will be a succession of blossoms and peppers in all stages of maturity throughout the season if you cultivate and mulch heavily

GREEN PEPPERS

to keep the soil moist and warm. The unharvested fruits eventually turn red and become a little milder in taste.

When gathering peppers, do not tear them off the vine because that injures the plant. Instead, cut them with a knife, close to the stem. Before frost, harvest and store peppers in a slatted or perforated container filled with dry sand in temperatures between 35° and 55°, where they should remain fresh for two to three months. Or they may be frozen, canned, or pickled.

Peppers are high in vitamins A, B, and C and low in calories, unless you prepare them with the following recipe, which is delicious served with roast lamb. It also makes a nice hostess present.

Pepper Jelly

With fresh or basket-stored peppers,
   prepare the following:
¾ cup bell peppers, ground
¼ cup hot peppers, ground
6½ cups sugar
1½ cups apple-cider vinegar
1 6-ounce bottle Certo (no substitutes)
1½ teaspoons red or green food coloring

Grind the bell and hot peppers together, saving the juice. In a large kettle, mix the juices, sugar, and apple-cider vinegar; bring to boil and cook 5 minutes. Cool 5 minutes and add Certo and food coloring. Makes 7½ regular jelly glasses. Seal with paraffin. (Do not try to double or triple the recipe.)

RADISHES

The word "radish" comes from the Latin word *radix,* meaning root, and that's exactly what a radish is—an edible root. It is one of the easiest crops to grow, but frequently the gardener is frustrated by lush top growth and no roots. When this happens it's usually because the seeds have been planted too closely and not thinned to at least an inch apart. Or the seeds may have been sown too late in the spring. Substantial root development depends on planting before the weather becomes hot, and on sufficient space for each top to develop a root that will not touch its neighbor. Radishes are another cool-weather crop and will go to seed under hot-summer sun; White Icicle is one of the few exceptions that adapts rather well to midsummer temperatures.

Red radishes such as Cherry Belle, Scarlet Globe, or Comet offer a cheerful beginning to your first vegetable crop. They can be harvested twenty-five to thirty days after planting the easy-to-handle seeds thinly, a half-inch deep in rows six inches apart in well-drained, friable soil with full sun. Successive sowings can be made throughout the spring, and again thirty days before frost is expected. Growing radishes is a good way to introduce gardening

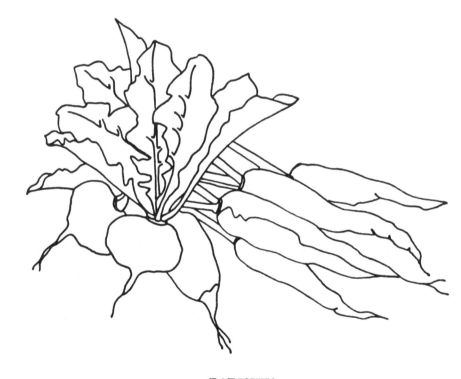

RADISHES

to children, because they don't have to wait very long for edible results!

Harvest mature radishes when they are one-half to one inch in diameter, otherwise they will become pithy, soft, and possibly wormy. White, yellow, and black radishes grow larger, take longer to mature, and have a stronger flavor than the red varieties. When planting in containers, remember that the more exotic species need more depth. A half-ounce package of radish seeds will sow fifty feet. Five days after planting, tender green shoots will appear, and that's the time to spread wood ashes or used tea leaves around the plants to repel maggots. Radishes are often planted around melons, cucumbers, and squash to deter the striped beetles that relish vine crops.

Before frost comes, store the late-summer crop as you would other root vegetables, in a basket of sand in a cool place.

Radishes, containing vitamins B and C, are quite interesting when cooked. They become milder in flavor than when they are raw, and resemble the turnip in taste. The Chinese have served them in cooked dishes for centuries. Try this recipe for a starter.

Radish Roots Supreme

1½ pounds radishes, sliced thinly
¾ teaspoon salt
¼ teaspoon pepper
¼ teaspoon dried tarragon
¼ teaspoon dried parsley
vegetable oil

Coat frying pan with vegetable oil. Add radishes and simmer gently with the other ingredients. Cook until just soft. Serves 6.

SPINACH

Spinach is so hardy it can be planted as soon as the ground can be worked in the spring, with continuous sowings every two weeks until early May and again in late summer. Seeds planted a half-inch deep in drills of well-drained, fertile, limy soil with sufficient moisture should provide an ample crop of green leaves for cooking, salads, canning, and freezing.

Rows planted fourteen inches apart, with plants spaced four or five inches apart, will be ready for harvest forty-two to seventy days later, depending on the variety planted. As the spinach matures, use the outer leaves for salads. The center will keep producing new leaves for cooking or preserving, and then will flower and bolt. An ounce of seeds will sow a seventy-five- to hundred-foot row. Allow forty feet for a family of four, but add another row or two if you plan to preserve (it is a very short-lived crop).

For late-summer plantings, select a blight-resistant variety such as Winter Bloomsdale or America. Both are heavy yielders with smooth rather than crinkly leaves. The fall crop can be left in the garden heavily mulched

113

SPINACH

with straw. Pick the greens, delectable both cooked and in salads, all winter long for a healthy addition of A, B, and C vitamins to your diet. Come spring, the crop will begin growing again. Those who prefer spinach to any other vegetable should try the New Zealand type, which can be grown all summer by allowing a little more space between the rows.

To freeze, wash the leaves and remove the stems. Boil a minute, drain, chill, and pack in plastic bags. Place in the freezer until ready to use. The following recipe is better prepared a day ahead.

Savory Chopped Spinach

1 8-ounce package frozen garden spinach
1 3-ounce package cream cheese (softened)
3 slices lean bacon
½ cup sour cream
1 tablespoon dried minced onions
1 tablespoon horseradish
salt to taste

Cook spinach until tender. Drain and chop. Cook and crumble the bacon. Add all ingredients to spinach and mix well. Place in lightly buttered casserole dish and bake in 350° oven for 25 minutes or until hot. Serves 4.

SQUASH

Growing squash is rewarding for several reasons: compared to some other vegetables, they are less demanding; mature quickly; taste divine; freeze, can, or store well; and come in both summer and winter varieties. What more can you ask?

The most common summer squashes include yellow crookneck and straightneck, and green or yellow zucchini. Bush varieties require less space than runners but are more susceptible to disease. Sow seeds directly into sandy soil enriched with compost and manure after the soil has become completely warm. Squashes grow beautifully in well-drained, rich, light soil with full sunlight. Water generously and never allow the ground to become dry or crusty.

A half-ounce of seeds will sow a hundred feet, although squash is more often planted by putting five seeds in four-inch-high hills spaced four feet apart. When the plants are two inches high, remove two of the weaker plants and either discard or transplant. Three abundantly bearing plants will feed a family of four.

Some gardeners plant melon or radish seeds around

SUMMER SQUASH

squash to ward off enemies. Other theories hold that cigarette or wood ashes sprinkled around individual plants after they sprout are effective pesticides. Stem borers are particular nuisances just when the vines promise great production. If a plant suddenly collapses and wilts, look for sawdustlike debris on the vines where the borers have entered. If the main vine has not been attacked, cut off the infested shoot. Otherwise slit the main stem, remove the borers with tweezers, and cover the incision with soil. Hopefully new roots will form. A daily check for borers is worth the effort. They are easily identified by their unpleasant odor after they have been "squashed"!

Curiously, the male and female flowers on members of the cucumber and squash family are easily distinguished. The male flower has a powdery pollen and the female has a baby fruit at the base of its petals. Both sexes are necessary for pollination and the development of fruit. If undeveloped fruit appears, blame the bees—they goofed!

Harvest the summer yellows at the peak of perfection, when they are about four inches long. Zucchini may remain on the vine until six to eight inches long, or when the vines are soft enough for your fingernail to indent without much pressure. Another indication of harvesttime is when the flower falls off the tip. It's tempting to leave the vegetables on the vine until they become gigantic showpieces; however, they can lose flavor, become pulpy, and retard the other fruits beginning to mature on the same vine. Summer squash is most delectable when cooked immediately after picking. It can be frozen but, because of its high water content, becomes limp when defrosted.

Winter squash varieties popular with home-gardening enthusiasts include acorn, butternut, and Blue Hubbard. Their culture is the same as for summer squash

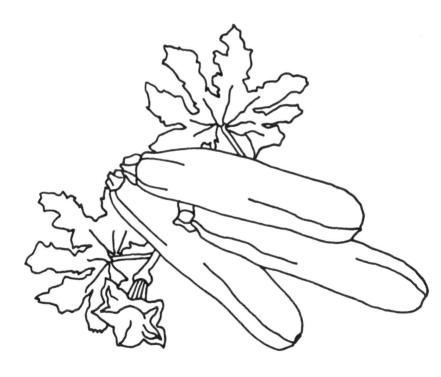

ZUCCHINI SQUASH

except for harvesting. They should remain in the garden until just before frost or until their rinds become hard and brittle. If the rinds have not hardened, and frost threatens, gather them with part of the stem still attached. Avoid bruising, because this causes rot. Lay each squash on a bed of straw and rotate them in the sun for ten days, sheltering from both cold and rain. Store ripened squashes in a dry, dark area between 45° and 55°, and they should keep well into the winter.

Summer squash needs blanching for only a minute or two before freezing (a half-minute if grated), but winter squash must be fully cooked first. It may also be canned. Squash contains vitamin A and is a tasty supplement to your dinner table.

Zucchini for Two

1½ cups grated unpeeled zucchini
1 teaspoon salt
¼ tablespoon tarragon (dried)
1 tablespoon lemon juice
½ cup sour cream yogurt
¼ teaspoon ground pepper
1 tablespoon dry white wine

Remove grated garden-fresh zucchini from freezer and place in boiling water for 5 minutes. Drain the liquid through a strainer. Return the zucchini to the saucepan and add remaining ingredients, blending well. Make a day in advance to let the flavors mingle. Heat gently before serving.

To freeze winter squash, peel off rind, remove seeds and stringy pulp, cut into small pieces, and boil until soft

BUTTERNUT SQUASH

(about fifteen minutes). Pour off water, mash until smooth, cool, and place in freezer until ready to use.

Buttery Butternut Squash

6 cups cooked frozen squash
½ cup pecans
½ cup pure maple syrup
½ teaspoon cinnamon
¼ teaspoon nutmeg
salt to taste

Defrost squash by placing in top of double boiler. When squash is hot, add all ingredients and mix well. Serves 8.

TOMATOES

The delicious, nutritious tomato is the most widely grown home-garden vegetable in the United States. Excluding lettuce, it is probably the most frequently used ingredient in salads. When tomatoes were first found by the conquistadores in South America, the fruit was believed to be poisonous because of its striking resemblance to the deadly nightshade, a poisonous relative common in Europe. But once this was disproved, tomatoes rapidly gained favor as "apples of gold" in Italy and "apples of love" in France.

Later in your gardening career, experiment with starting plants from seeds (see pages 31–36). For now, select sturdy, dark-green plants with stems the diameter of a pencil and no yellow or pale-green leaves. Eight plants of a heavy-bearing variety such as Moreton Hybrid, Beefsteak, Valiant, Burpee's Big Early, or Big Boy will yield about two hundred pounds. After the frost date in your locality, plant in a well-drained area that receives at least six hours of direct sun. Tomatoes like water, but not wet feet. Soak the garden weekly for about an hour with a hose if it hasn't rained.

TOMATOES

The plants should be two to three feet apart with the first few nodes (a swelling that looks like a knot) buried. Lightly sprinkle an organic fertilizer around each plant, and water well. If wood ashes are available, scatter them on top of the fertilizer to ward off flea beetles. A 2- by 2-inch paper collar around the base of the stem and a half-inch beneath the soil discourages cutworms. Intersperse with parsley, which repels flies; marigolds as a border add color and trap aphids and nematodes.

It's advisable not to plant tomatoes in last year's potato or tomato patch or near this year's potato or corn plantings. Tomatoes exposed to tobacco may develop a mosaic virus, so don't handle the vines after smoking or smoke in the tomato garden.

Each plant should have a sturdy stake or other support firmly anchored right next to it when you plant (if you insert the support later, you might damage the root system). Gardeners have devised a number of different supports, but in your first year why not start with purchased poles as high as the mature height of the variety? Fasten the vine to the pole as it grows to protect it from wind and storm damage.

Tying the vines to the stakes should be done carefully. First, knot the soft cord, strip of sheet, or nylon ties on the stake and then loop around the main stem before tying the ends together. Don't make the first knot on the vine because it could squeeze it and interfere with the transference of water and nutrients. Staking and tying the vines keep the fruit off the ground, where it can rot and attract bugs. We place our poles in a tripod position, which adds a touch of Indian romance to the garden. If space is short, train tomatoes up a trellis or grow them as a border along the side of the house. Some growers prefer a cylindrical wire cage three to six feet tall made from four to six inch mesh—large enough to get your hands through to pick the tomatoes. Lazy gardeners buy "tomato towers" that almost eliminate the need for tying.

When the first flowers begin to appear, add another light dressing of organic fertilizer, cultivate, and water—and watch what happens!

Some gardeners prune suckers—shoots that appear in the joints between the main and leaf stems—claiming the plant will thereby produce larger tomatoes. I've tried pruning and not pruning and find the results comparable. A frugal gardener, however, can plant the suckers and get a whole new crop if his growing season is sufficiently long. Let the suckers grow at least eight inches long and then carefully cut them from the mother plant. Plant immediately at least four inches deep in a prepared bed. Firm the soil well around the shoots and give them plenty of water. Keep the ground moist and protect the new plants with a perforated covering, such as a pint basket, against direct sunrays for about a week.

If tomato plants have been put in the garden around the middle of May, they will reach full glory early in August and continue yielding until frost. When frost is predicted, harvest all the green tomatoes for pickling or wrap in newspaper and place in a dark area, where some may ripen. Leave the tomatoes that have started coloring on the vines, uproot the whole plant, and hang upside down in a warm place that is not too dry.

Mulching the ground around tomatoes is important as the weather gets hotter and the ground warms up. Mulch helps retain moisture, adds nutrients, discourages weeds, and controls slugs and rot. Always keep the garden free of weeds and don't apply the 2-inch layer of mulch before the plants flower, as it can retard fruit formation. When all the tomatoes have ripened, place the vines on your compost heap; however, if there is any trace of disease, burn or discard them.

There are at least 150 varieties of tomatoes listed in garden catalogs, including early bloomers, gold-fruited, and dwarfs called cherry tomatoes, which are excellent in salads or as an hors d'oeuvre. If dwarf varieties are planted in the garden rather than in containers (see page 37), they should be spaced eighteen to twenty inches apart and staked. Big Boy, a hybrid, is our favorite full-size plant because it bears large, smooth-skinned, meaty tomatoes and has a rather long bearing season, extending from July until frost. Home-grown tomatoes are a fine source of vitamins A and C and can be eaten broiled, baked, stewed, and juiced, in salads, and as stock in soups and casseroles. Once you've raised this vegetable, you'll never again want to be without your own supply.

Tomatoes are usually preserved by canning because they are the easiest and safest vegetable to can and because most freezing literature does not include them. Their high water content makes them mushy when defrosted— unacceptable for salads or other uncooked dishes. It is possible, however, to freeze tomatoes for stewing, soup, sauce, and juice.

To prepare tomatoes for stewing, remove the skins and any blemishes, cut in half, place in a kettle of cold water, and add sugar to taste. When the water boils, drain and put the tomatoes into plastic containers, leaving an inch at the top for expansion. When they are cool, place them in the freezer.

Freezing tomatoes for sauce or juice takes only minutes. Wash and quarter whole unpeeled tomatoes, removing only blemishes and core. Place in blender and puree until smooth. Fill pint containers, leaving one inch headspace.

Tomato Sauce

1 pint frozen tomato puree
1 small onion, chopped
½ green pepper, chopped
sprig of fresh parsley
1 bay leaf
1 garlic bud
¼ teaspoon oregano
salt and pepper to taste
1 scant tablespoon sugar
⅛ cup Parmesan cheese
½ pound ground meat
1 small can tomato paste
1 tablespoon flour
3 tablespoons butter
cooked spaghetti for 3

Heat tomato puree. Add next 8 ingredients, blending well. Add flour to melted butter, making a paste. Gradually add the tomato mixture, stirring constantly until thickened. Add cheese and tomato paste. Brown meat in separate pan and add to the sauce. Simmer for at least an hour, adding water as necessary. Remove bay leaf and garlic bud before pouring over cooked spaghetti. Serves 3.

INDEX

Almond Green Beans in Brown Butter, 46
aromatic plants as insect repellents, 28–29. *See also* garlic *and* marigolds
ashes, wood, 16, 17, 19, 65, 89, 105, 127

basil, 28, 30, 71
beans, bush, 29, 38, 43–46; lima, 29, 46–49; yellow (wax), 43
beets, 29, 51–54; as pH indicator, 17–18
blanching (in cooking), 103, 121
blanching leeks and onions, 94, 96
bonemeal, 17, 35, 57
Bouquet Garni, 85–86
Braised Lettuce, 90
Bread-and-Butter Pickles, 67–68
Buttery Butternut Squash, 123

cabbage, 29, 38, 55–59
canning, basic hot-pack method of, 11, 48
carrots, 29, 37, 61–63
Chinese Pickled Beets, 53–54
chives, 28, 30, 71–74
cold frames, 32, 35–36
companion planting of vegetables, 27–28, 61, 69; *chart,* 29–30

compost, use of, 16, 17, 65
compost heap, developing, 18–19
containers for indoor seed starting, 32; for outdoor gardening, 37–38
Creamed Onions, 93
cress, garden, 30, 31, 74–76
cross-pollination, 31
cucumbers, 29, 37, 38, 65–68

dill, 30, 74
drainage, importance of, in container planting, 38
dried blood, 17, 28
droughts, 20
drying herbs, 69

fertilizers, organic (nonchemical), 16–17
following crops, 21
freezing vegetables, 11, 45–46, 94, 115, 119, 129; herbs, 70, 78

garlic, 28, 67
Green Goddess Dressing, 96
greens, beet, 51, 53

hardening process for seedlings, 32
Herb Croutons, 85
Herb Vinegar, 85

herbs, 11, 30, 37, 38, 69–86; indoors, 39
Hot-Packed Canning for Lima Beans, 48

indoor planting, 31–36, 89, 105
insect pests, 10, 27–28, 51, 57, 67, 89, 111, 119, 127

ladybugs, 28
leeks, 93–94
lettuce, 29, 87–90
lime, applying, 16, 19, 76, 105

manure, types of, 16
marigolds, 28, 29, 31, 57, 67, 127
marjoram, 30, 76
marking placement of seeds, 19–20
Mint-Glazed Carrots, 63
mulching vegetables, 19, 53, 89, 93, 105, 128

nitrogen, 17, 43, 48

onions, 28, 29, 67, 91–93
oregano, 76
organic gardening, 10, 69. *See also* repellents, natural

parsley, 30, 78, 127
peas, 29, 99–103; snow or Chinese, 99, 103
peppers, sweet, 29, 37, 38, 105–107
pesticides, organic, 27–28, 57, 67, 71, 119
pH of soil, determining, 16–17
phosphorus, 17
planting mixes, soilless, 38
Pork Chop Casserole, 59
potassium (potash), 17, 105
praying mantises, 28
preparing soil in garden sites, 15, 16–19

Radish Roots Supreme, 111
radishes, 29, 37, 109–111

repellents, natural insect and disease, 27–28, 57, 67, 71, 111, 119, 127
Rich Leek Soup, 94
rosemary, 28, 30, 80

sample kitchen-garden plans, 20–21
Sauerkraut, 58
Savory Chopped Spinach, 115
scallions, 29, 94–96
slugs, controlling, 28, 128
Snow Peas à l'Américaine, 103
soaking or freezing seeds before planting, 45, 71, 78, 101
soil mixtures, 18, 38, 43, 65, 78
space requirement for vegetable plot, 9, 15, 18, 21
spinach, 11, 29, 113–115
squash, 29, 117–123
storing vegetables in winter, 53, 57–58, 63, 70, 107, 121
successive sowing, 38, 45, 51, 65, 87, 93, 109, 113
Succulent Succotash, 49
suckers, pruning and replanting, on tomato plants, 128
sunny location, importance of, 15, 16, 32, 38, 70, 87

tarragon, 30, 80
thyme, 28, 30, 83
Tomato Sauce, 130
tomatoes, 29, 37, 38, 125–130
tools, gardening, 16
transplanting seedlings, 32, 35–36, 57

vinegar, tarragon, 80

watering, 20, 38, 76, 117, 125; seedlings, 32, 36
weeding, 16, 38, 45, 93, 128. *See also* mulching

Zucchini for Two, 121